Transportation

Deborah Cannarella

Jane Fournier

The Rourke Press
Vero Beach, Florida

Photo credits

All photos copyright ©: Airbus Industrie, p. 28 top; AP/Worldwide Photos, pp. 19 bottom, 27 middle and 30 bottom (The Virginia-Pilot, HO); Corbis, pp. 13 top, 16 bottom, 17 top; Corbis/Austrian Archives, p. 20; Corbis/Baldwin H. Ward, pp. 12 bottom, 14 bottom; Corbis/Bettmann, pp. 9 bottom (Da Vinci), 11 bottom, 12 top, 13 bottom, 15 top, 17 bottom, 18 bottom, 24 top, 25 middle; Corbis/Museum of Flight, pp. 21 top, 22 top; Delorme, p. 25 top; Ed Eckstein/Corbis, p. 10 top; Ford Motor Company, pp. 26–27 and 30 top; Grant Smith/Corbis, p. 21 bottom; Hulton Getty/Liaison Agency, p. 23 top; NASA, pp. 24 bottom, 29 bottom, 27 top and 31 bottom; North Wind Pictures, pp. 6 top, 7 top, 4 bottom and 7 bottom, 8 top and bottom, 14 top, 15 bottom; PhotoDisc, p. 3; Princess Cruises, pp. 26 bottom and 28 bottom; Raytheon Systems Company, p. 29 top; Reuters/Denis Ballbouse ARC/Archive Photos, p. 1 and 25 bottom; Stock Montage, Inc., pp. 6 bottom, 4–5 and 9 top, 10 bottom, 4 top and 11 top, 16 top, 18 top, 19 top; UPI/Corbis-Bettmann, pp. 22 bottom, 23 bottom. Cover: Street car photo copyright Corbis/Bettman; all other images and introduction page image PhotoDisc.

© 1999 The Rourke Press, Inc.

Printed in the United States of America

An Editorial Directions Book
Book design and production by Criscola Design

Library of Congress Cataloging-in-Publication Data

Cannarella, Deborah.
    Transportation / Deborah Cannarella, Jane Fournier.
    p. cm. — (Into the next millennium)
    Summary : Surveys the history of transportation from floating logs to the space shuttle and speculates about future methods of travel.
    ISBN 1-57103-276-2
    1. Transportation Juvenile literature. [1. Transportation—History.] I. Fournier, Jane, 1955– . II. Title. III. Series.
    TA1149.C36 1999
    629.04–dc21
                                                99-25471
                                                CIP

Introduction

The history of the human race is a story of great discoveries and amazing achievements. Since ancient times, people have found creative solutions to problems, met impossible challenges, and turned visions into reality. Each of these remarkable people—and each of their contributions—changed the world they lived in forever. Together, they created the world we know and live in today.

The six books in this series—*Medicine, Transportation, Communication, Exploration, Engineering,* and *Sports*—present a timeline of the great discoveries and inventions that have shaped our world. As you travel from ancient to modern times, you will discover the many ways in which people have worked to heal sickness, shape materials, share information, explore strange places, and achieve new goals. Although they worked with many different tools, their goal was always the same: to improve our quality of life.

As we enter the twenty-first century, we will continue to build on what each generation of people before us has created and discovered. With the knowledge they have given us, we will discover new ways to build, heal, communicate, discover, and achieve. We will continue to change the world in ways we can only begin to imagine.

From the *Past...*

3500 B.C.

Early people probably first traveled by water on logs or in canoes carved from tree trunks. By 3500 B.C., Egyptians made rafts from the reeds that grew along the Nile River. Drawings in Egyptian tombs more than 5,000 years old show **sailboats** with one mast.

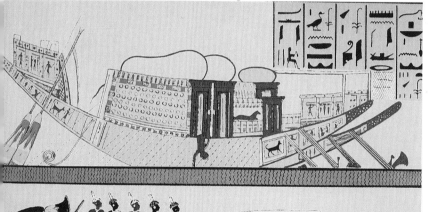

Early wheels—some dating about 5,000 years ago—were made of stone, solid wood, or pieces of wood joined together. Wheels with spokes were invented about 2000 B.C.

3000 B.C.

To travel by sea, Egyptians built sturdy wooden boats. These boats had a rudder, or large paddle, to make steering possible. They were powered by sails and by people rowing with oars. Most of these early Egyptian boats, called **galleys,** had one square sail and one row of oarsmen.

2000 B.C.

People were riding **horses** more than 5,000 years ago. By about 2000 B.C., warriors in Babylonia and other ancient cultures rode on horseback for more speed and control during battle.

After the invention of the wheel, people used carts drawn by animals to travel and carry goods.

700 B.C.

The Phoenicians were important sea traders. They built strong ships from the wood of tall cedar trees. These ships had large, square sails that caught the wind as men rowed with oars. The Phoenicians built the first **bireme**— a ship with two rows of oars on either side of the boat, which made it travel very fast.

27 B.C.

The ancient Romans used open carts called **chariots** for travel and racing. The two-wheeled vehicles were pulled by two or more horses. The chariot had no seat, so the driver had to stand. For special events, as many as 10 horses might lead the chariot— and sometimes even dogs and ostriches!

The Appian Way, begun in 312 B.C., is one of the longest ancient roads ever built. It ran from what is now Rome, Italy, to the Adriatic Sea—410 miles (255 km). The strong, smooth road was made of layers of stone and lava blocks. Much of the famous road still exists today.

100

The earliest steam engine was made by the inventor Hero of Alexandria. His device was called the **aeolipile.** Water was heated in a tank to create steam. The hot steam flowed out of two curved tubes with enough power to turn a hollow sphere. The machine had no use—but the design of jet engines hundreds of years later was based on Hero's idea.

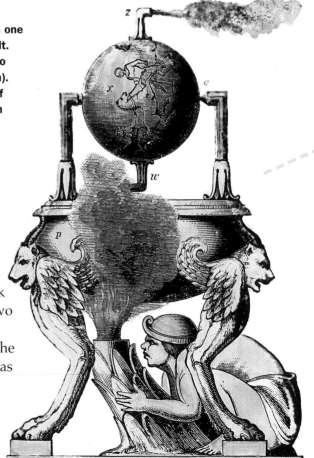

1400

During the early Middle Ages (fifth to eighth centuries), roads in Europe were not often used and were not well maintained. When people traveled, they rode horses or mules. By the fifteenth century, travelers rode in many types of **wagons and carriages** on an improved and expanded system of roads.

1487

Artist and scientist Leonardo da Vinci made the first drawings of **flying machines.** This sketch was one of da Vinci's designs for the helicopter. The person standing on pedals at the center of the machine worked the wings.

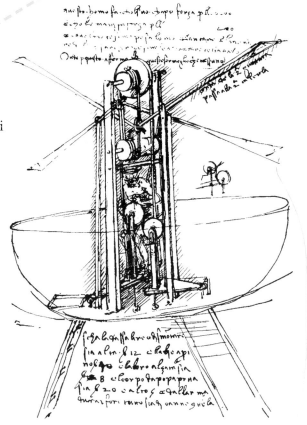

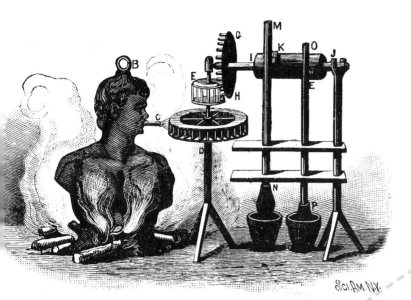

1629

The **simple steam turbine** was designed by Italian engineer Giovanni Branca. A powerful jet of steam turned the blades of a wheel, which caused other wheels to move at high speed. His machine provided power for a stone-crushing mill.

The steam engine built by Thomas Newcomen in 1712 worked with an up-and-down, pumping motion. In 1784, James Watts built an engine that moved in a strong, circular motion and was able to turn gear wheels.

1653

In 1620, Dutch engineer Cornelis Drebbel built a submarine propelled by oars. Thirty-three years later, a Frenchman named de Son attempted to build the first **mechanically powered submarine.** The windup motor, however, was not strong enough to turn the paddlewheel at the center of the boat.

David Bushnell's submarine of 1775, named the *Turtle*, was made of oak and operated by hand-cranked screws.

1783

Brothers Joseph-Michel and Jacques-Étienne Montgolfier discovered that if hot air were trapped inside a paper or fabric bag, the bag would rise. Their first **hot-air balloon** rose about 3,000 feet (915 m) and hovered for about 10 minutes. Three months later, the brothers launched another balloon—with a sheep, rooster, and duck as passengers! Later that year, the first human passengers sailed over Paris.

In 1801, American engineer Robert Fulton designed and built the *Nautilus* submarine. To travel on the surface of the water, the boat had a mast and sail. Underwater, the submarine was powered by a hand-turned propeller.

1801

Richard Trevithick of England built and drove the first **steam-powered road carriage** in 1801. By 1868, people in Britain were traveling in steam-powered personal carriages (left) that could reach speeds of 20 miles (32 km) per hour. A steam automobile, known as a Stanley Steamer, took the world speed record in 1906 at 127 miles (205 km) per hour.

1807

The first **commercial steamboat** was designed by American engineer Robert Fulton. On its launch in 1807, the *North River Steamboat* traveled 150 miles (240 km) up the Hudson River in 32 hours. It took sailboats four days to make the same trip. The wood-burning steamboat was later renamed the *Clermont.*

In 1804, Richard Trevithick built the world's first steam-powered railway locomotive. It hauled 10 tons of iron and 70 people along a 10-mile (16-km) railway in Wales.

1813

William Hedley built the first **commercial steam locomotive.** The four-wheeled locomotive weighed 8 tons—and was too heavy for the rails. The design was changed to eight wheels to distribute the weight. Headley's invention, *Puffing Billy,* pulled trucks about 5 miles (8 km) from a coal mine to the English docks.

1816

The first bicycle, called a Hobby Horse, was built by Baron Karl de Drais de Sauerbrun. It was made of wood and had no pedals. The rider moved by pushing his feet against the ground. In 1839, Kirkpatrick Macmillan, a Scottish blacksmith, invented the first **pedal-powered bicycle.** His machine, called a Boneshaker (below), had an iron frame and wheels with iron rims. The rider swung cranks at the front of the bike with each foot.

On May 31, 1868, James Moore won the first recorded bicycle race, which was held in France. Moore's bike weighed 160 pounds (73 kg) and had solid rubber tires and ball bearings. He traveled 83 miles (134 km) in 10 hours 25 minutes.

By 1931, electric elevators in the Empire State Building in New York City traveled at the speed of 1,200 feet (365 m)—about 102 stories—per minute.

1854

Elisha Graves Otis invented a safety device that made the first **passenger elevator** possible. His "safety hoist" (left) was designed to keep the elevator from falling if the lifting chain or rope broke. The first passenger elevator, driven by steam power, was put into service in a department store in New York City in 1857. It climbed five stories in less than one minute.

1863

The first **subway** in the world was the Metropolitan Railway in London. The "underground" ran for 3.75 miles (6 km). Steam locomotives carried 9,500,000 passengers in the first year. The first electric underground railway—also known as the tube—began operation in London in 1890.

George Pullman introduced special train cars so passengers could sleep during overnight journeys. To provide more comforts to train passengers, he later introduced the Pullman dining car.

1867

German engineers Nikolaus Otto and Eugene Langen built the first successful **internal combustion engine**. It was fueled by coal gas. In an internal combustion engine, fuel burns inside the engine itself—rather than in a separate tank, as in a steam engine.

1869

The first **motorcycle** was a Boneshaker bicycle fitted with a small steam engine (right). It was built by Sylvester Howard Roper. The first motor tricycle was built in 1884 by Englishman Edward Butler. German inventor Gottlieb Daimler built the first motorcycle powered by a gasoline engine in 1885.

The Union Pacific and the Central Pacific Railroads were joined in 1869—creating the first transcontinental railroad across the United States. After 6 $1/2$ years, 1,800 miles (2,900 km) of track had been laid by hand. The last spike was driven on May 10 in northern Utah.

1880

In 1880, American inventor Thomas Alva Edison tested a small **electric railway engine** in Menlo Park, California. In 1895, the first electric locomotives were put into service by the Baltimore and Ohio Railroad. Edison's electric locomotive traveled on electrified railroads in Massachusetts, New Jersey, and Maryland.

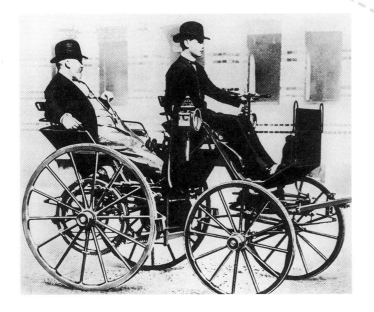

1886

In 1885, Gottlieb Daimler and Wilhelm Maybech tested their gasoline-powered version of the internal combustion engine on a bicycle. In 1886, they tried it on a four-wheeled carriage. Their "horseless carriage" reached a speed of 10 miles (16 km) per hour. By 1889, a French company was building bodies for the engines—and the first **automobiles** were offered for sale.

In 1890, inventor Clément Ader launched his steam-powered, bat-winged monoplane, called the *Eole*. It was the first full-sized airplane to leave the ground under its own power.

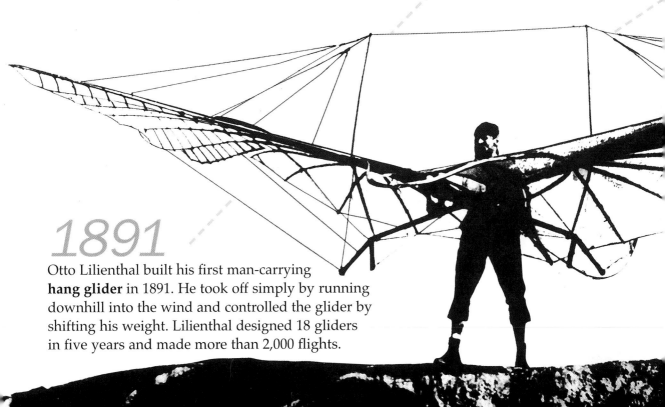

1891

Otto Lilienthal built his first man-carrying **hang glider** in 1891. He took off simply by running downhill into the wind and controlled the glider by shifting his weight. Lilienthal designed 18 gliders in five years and made more than 2,000 flights.

1898

John Philip Holland designed and built the first submarine accepted by the U.S. Navy. The **Holland submarine** was powered by a gasoline engine while traveling on the surface of the water and by electric motors while underwater.

In 1804, George Cayley built the first model of a successful man-carrying glider. In 1853, he launched the first full-sized glider on the first manned flight.

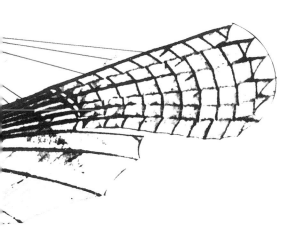

1900

In 1888, Frank Sprague—who worked with Thomas Edison—opened the first citywide system of **electric streetcars** in Richmond, Virginia. The streetcars were powered by overhead electrified wires. These streetcars, also called trolley cars, became important methods of travel in cities and growing towns. By 1915, there were 45,000 miles (72,000 km) of streetcar lines in the United States.

1900

Count Ferdinand von Zeppelin flew the first rigid "air ship" over Germany. The ship, known as a **zeppelin,** could travel up to 20 miles (32 km) per hour. The famous *Graf Zeppelin* was completed in 1928 and made 590 flights between 1928 and 1936—including a trip around the world in 10 days in 1929.

In 1907, Louis-Charles Bréguet flew the first working helicopter. It rose 2 feet (.6 m)—but was still attached to the ground! That year, Paul Cornu's free-flying helicopter rose 1 foot (.3 m) above the ground for 20 seconds.

1903

Brothers Orville and Wilbur Wright flew their **gasoline-powered airplane** in 1903. Their biplane (two-winged plane) was made of wood, wire, and cloth. In their first successful flight, Orville flew 120 feet (37 m) in 12 seconds. During the summer of 1904, the Wright brothers took off 105 times. One flight lasted a record 5 minutes 4 seconds.

1911

Glen Curtiss fitted floats to one of his land biplanes and flew it off the water. He had built the first **seaplane.** In 1919, one of his "flying boats" crossed the Atlantic Ocean for the first time. By the late 1920s, seaplanes were the largest and fastest aircraft in the world.

Richard Pearse first flew his gasoline-powered monoplane in New Zealand in 1902.

1913

In 1908, Henry Ford designed and built the **Model T,** the first automobile made for the general public. The Model T, or Tin Lizzie, began to be manufactured in 1913. Ford was the first to use assembly-line production to cut costs. For the first time, many people could afford to buy cars. By 1927, Ford sold more than 15 million of his "horseless carriages."

In 1923, to improve safety in Cleveland, Ohio, Garrett Augustus Morgan invented the first automatic traffic signal. His signal was a T-shaped pole with three positions: Stop, Go, and All Stop. The third position made it possible for people to cross the streets safely.

1924

Germany built the first **express highways,** called autobahns. Sections were built on concrete stilts above the ground to avoid damaging the farmland below. Today, Germany's autobahn system includes about 6,500 miles (10,500 km) of highways.

In 1919, John Alcock and Arthur Whitten Brown made the first nonstop flight across the Atlantic Ocean—from Newfoundland, Canada, to County Galway, Ireland. Their flight took 16 hours 12 minutes. In 1927, Charles A. Lindbergh made the first nonstop solo flight across the Atlantic Ocean. His flight from New York to Paris, in the monoplane the *Spirit of St. Louis,* took 33 1/2 hours.

1926

Henry Ford, maker of the Model T automobile, built one of the first all-metal **passenger airplanes.** With three engines, the Ford Trimotor could fly higher and faster than other aircraft—up to 130 miles (209 km) per hour. The plane, also called the Tin Goose, had 12 passenger seats, a cabin, and a room for a flight attendant. The first flight attendants were nurses who served meals and helped airsick passengers.

The U.S. Post Office started airmail service in 1918, using aircraft and pilots it borrowed from the Army. Three months later, the Post Office hired its own pilots and bought its own airplanes. The first airmail route was between Washington, D.C., and New York City.

1939

In 1909, Igor Sikorsky began to experiment with Leonardo da Vinci's ideas for a **helicopter.** In 1939, he flew the first test flight of his small, single-rotor (single-blade) helicopter. Two years later, his craft set a flight record of 1 hour 32.4 seconds.

1952

The first **passenger jet airliner** was the British de Havilland Comet, which began service in 1952. America's first passenger jetliner, the Boeing 707, went into service in 1958.

In 1945, Robert Fulton Jr. created the *Airphibian*—a flying car. He was not the first to create a vehicle that could travel on land and in the air, but his craft was the first approved for production by the U.S. government. Only eight were built.

Japan's high-speed rail line, the Shinkansen, began passenger service in 1964. Its fast trains, called bullet trains, travel at a speed of 130 miles (210 km) to 160 miles (260 km) per hour.

1954

The USS *Nautilus* was the first **nuclear-powered submarine** built by the U.S. Navy. It was powered by steam from a nuclear reactor. The submarine could travel underwater for long periods at speeds greater than 20 knots (23 miles or 34 km per hour). In 1958, the *Nautilus* made a historic cruise under the ice cap of the North Pole.

1955

A **hovercraft** floats above land or water on a cushion of air. British designer Christopher Cockerell invented the air-cushioned vehicle in 1955. His hovercraft SR.N1 first crossed the English Channel in 1959. The first passenger service using hovercraft began in 1965.

In 1947, American test pilot Charles Yeager was the first man to fly faster than the speed of sound—at the rate of about 662 miles (1,065 km) per hour. His aircraft was the rocket-powered Bell X-1.

In 1939, the Heinkel He 178 was the first jet aircraft to fly. Its engines were developed by Hans von Ohain of Germany.

1970

The success of the jet airplane engine rapidly increased the popularity of air travel. In 1964, the Boeing Company introduced the **Boeing 727,** which could carry 100 passengers. In 1970, the company launched its four-engined "jumbo jet." The Boeing 747 could carry up to 500 passengers—twice what any other passenger airline could carry at that time.

Paul MacCready designed and built the first solar-powered airplane. His *Solar Challenger* had more than 16,000 solar cells mounted on the wings. In 1981, pilot Stephen Ptacek flew the 210-pound (95-km) aircraft across the English Channel in 5 hours 23 minutes.

1976

The Concorde, the first **supersonic** (faster than sound) **airliner,** made its first flight in 1969. It first provided regular passenger service in 1976. The British- and French-built aircraft can travel at 2.5 times the speed of sound. The Concorde can fly across the Atlantic Ocean in three to four hours.

1981

The **space shuttle** is a spacecraft for carrying passengers from Earth to outer space and back again. The shuttle was designed to travel only to low Earth orbit (less than 298 miles or 480 km). The U.S. space shuttle *Columbia* completed its first mission in April 1981.

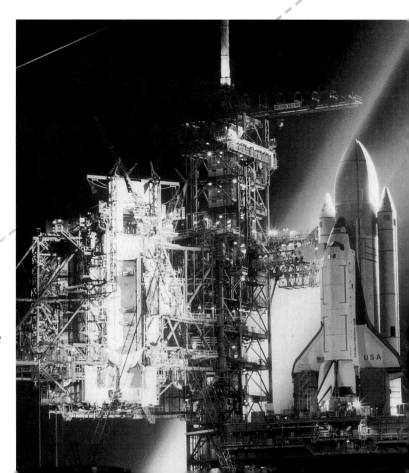

1993

The U.S. Air Force launched the twenty-fourth Navstar satellite into orbit in 1993. This completed a network of satellites known as the **Global Positioning System,** or GPS. The satellites send radio signals that are received on Earth. By comparing the distances to three different satellites, the receiver can pinpoint its latitude, longitude, and altitude. This navigation technology is even used in automobiles.

In 1984, Joe W. Kittinger made the first solo transatlantic balloon flight from Maine to Italy—a distance of 3,535 miles (5,688 km)—in his helium-filled balloon *Rosie O'Grady's Balloon of Peace.*

1999

Bertrand Piccard and Brian Jones flew the first nonstop balloon flight around the world. They were aloft for 19 days, traveling more than 26,500 miles (42,639 km). Their **state-of-the-art hot-air balloon** was 180 feet (55 m) high and large enough to hold the water from seven Olympic swimming pools. Three global positioning systems helped them navigate. Solar-powered batteries provided electricity.

...Into the *Future*

Double-decker airplanes.
Airplane manufacturers are designing double-decker, wide-bodied jets. With two full-sized passenger decks, one on top of the other, each plane will carry up to 650 passengers. Most airplanes seat fewer than 200 people. Double-decker planes will reduce airport and airspace traffic.

Supersize ships.
A new class of supersize cruise liners will offer vacationers all the entertainment and comforts found in a small city—shopping, movies, health clubs, and sports. These large, luxury ships can carry 2,600 passengers. Some are almost 1,000 feet (305 m) long and 200 feet (61 m) high.

Superfast ships.
New cargo ships may move freight twice as fast as conventional ships—and in any weather. The ships' hulls are designed to remain stable even in rough seas. They will travel at 40 knots (46 miles or 74 km per hour), making the trip from the United States to Europe in only four days.

People movers.
City planners are developing group rapid transit (GRT) and personal rapid transit (PRT) systems. Small, rail-mounted cars would each carry four or more people. In PRT systems, individual cars are available on demand. Both of these systems would reduce the traffic in busy cities.

Hyper-X planes.
Engineers are testing ways to make air travel cheaper and faster. Hypersonic (hyper-x) aircraft may be able to carry passengers around the world in record time. These would fly faster than Mach 5 (five times the speed of sound)—about 1 mile (1.6 km) per second. The plane's special air-breathing rocket engines will burn the oxygen in the air and liquid hydrogen as fuel.

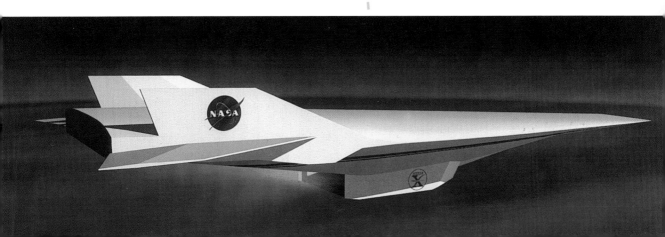

Electric cars.
To reduce the air pollution caused by automobile exhaust, more people will be driving electric cars that run on batteries. Eventually, scientists hope to develop electric cars powered by fuel cells. Fuel cells combine hydrogen and oxygen to make electricity and create no pollution. Fuel cells do not need to be recharged, as batteries do.

Maglevs.
A maglev (magnetic levitation) train does not ride on rails like a conventional train. Instead, the train is lifted off the rail and propelled forward by the forces between powerful magnets in the train and the guide rail underneath it. The maglev passenger train may be able to reach speeds of 310 miles (499 km) per hour safely and quietly.

Smart cars.
Engineers are developing computer-guided "smart" cars that drive themselves. These cars will maneuver safely through traffic and navigate to any destination. They receive information from magnets buried in the roads and from radar, cameras, and computers.

Next-generation shuttle.
Engineers are designing reusable space-launch vehicles—such as the X-33—that can transport people and supplies into space. These vehicles can reach orbit using their own engines. They will not need booster rockets as a space shuttle does. Next-generation shuttles may travel faster than Mach 15 (fifteen times the speed of sound).

Index

Aeolipile, 8

Airplanes
    All-metal passenger, 21
    Double-decker, 28
    Gasoline-powered, 18
    Hypersonic, 29
    and jet airliners, 22, 23
    and nonstop flights, 20
    Solar-powered, 24
    and the speed of sound, 23, 24
    Steam-powered, 16
    and the U.S. Post Office, 21

Autobahn, 20

Automobiles
    Computer-guided, 31
    Electric, 30
    First, 16
    First made for the general public, 19
    Flying, 22
    and Global Positioning Systems, 25
    Steam, 11

Bicycles, 13

Biremes, 7

Carriages
    "Horseless," 16, 19
    in the fifteenth century, 9
    Steam-powered, 11

Chariots, 8

Elevators, 13

Engines
    Internal combustion, 14
    Steam, 8, 10

Express highways, 20

Galleys, 6

Gliders, 16, 17

Helicopters
    Inspiration for, 9
    Free-flying, 18
    Single-blade, 21

Horses, 7

Hot-air balloons, 11, 25

Hovercrafts, 23

Group rapid transit systems, 29

Locomotives, *see trains*

Maglev, 30

Model T, 19, 21

Motorcycles, 15

Personal rapid transit systems, 29

Roads
    during the Middle Ages, 9
    in ancient Rome, 8

Sailboats, 6

Seaplanes, 19

Ships
    Superfast cargo, 28
    Supersized cruise liners, 28

Space Shuttle, 24, 31

Steamboats, 12

Streetcars, 17

Submarines
    and hand-turned propellers, 11
    Holland, 17
    Mechanically powered, 10
    Nuclear-powered, 22

Subways, 14

Traffic signals, 20

Trains
    Electric, 15
    and the first transcontinental railroad, 15
    High-speed, 22, 30
    and the Pullman dining car, 14
    Steam-powered, 12

Turbines, 10

Wagons, 9

Wheels, 6

Zepplins, 18

For further reading

Books

Berliner, Don. *Before the Wright Brothers.* Minneapolis: Lerner Publications, 1990.

Burns, Peggy, and Peter Chrisp. *Travel.* New York: Thomson Learning, 1995.

Gardner, Robert. *Transportation.* Brookfield, CT: Twenty First Century Books, 1995.

Richards, Roy. *Ships through Time.* Austin, TX: Raintree/Steck Vaughn, 1996.

Web sites

National Air and Space Museum

Information about airplanes throughout history
http://www.nasm.edu/GALLERIES/GAL102/gal102.html

The Transcontinental Railroad

Bureau of Land Management report on the history of American train travel
http://blm.gov/education/railroads/trans.html